Understanding, Life is Just a Place, and Other Original Poems

C. L. Saltz

Understanding, Life is Just a Place, and Other Original Poems
C. L. Saltz
ISBN 978-1-927967-68-3

Produced by IndieBookLauncher.com
www.IndieBookLauncher.com
Interior Design and Typesetting: Saul Bottcher
Cover photo: *Tranquility*, Saltz, C. L., 2012

The body text of this book is set in Adobe Caslon.

Notice of Rights
Copyright 2016 C. L. Saltz.

All rights reserved solely by the author. The author guarantees all contents are original and do not infringe upon the legal rights of any other person or work. No part of this book may be reproduced in any form without the permission of the author. The views expressed in this book are not necessarily those of the publisher.

Unless otherwise indicated, Bible quotations are taken from the King James Version.

Also Available
EPUB edition, ISBN 978-1-927967-69-0
Kindle edition, ISBN 978-1-927967-70-6

Heart of the Isle, ©2012 PhotosbyMeredith

~Contents~

Be Humble / Acknowledgements 9

Introduction 10

    Understanding 12

I. Believe 16

    Dreams... 20

    Be the You, You Want to Be 22

    Trust 26

    The Best You 28

    Believe 30

    Breaking Free 32

    Mold Your Own Way 35

    Looking Back 39

II. Love 42

    The Storyteller 46

    The Mirage 50

    Imagine 54

    Live Together 58

    Everyone Needs Someone 62

    Untrue Friendship 65

    Neighbors 68

(continued)

III. Listen 72

    Retirement..77

    Alone No More 81

    Right Where I Belong 83

    Peace 88

    Insight 91

IV. Grace 96

    Child of Mine..100

    Hope..102

    What If...104

    Wanderer 108

    Aloneness 110

    Trapped 113

    A Sinner's Prayer 117

V. Truth 120

    Happiness..124

    War...129

    Lies..133

    Get Your Cheer On 136

    Life's Real Meaning....................................142

    Rainy Day 145

    Life is Just a Place......................................148

VI. Faith 152
   It's Not Magic 156
   Mazical 159
   Chameleon 162
   I Look to You 167
   Trip to Heaven 169
   What Does it Take to Succeed 173
Summary.. 176
About the Author 177

Understanding and Other Poems

Be Humble

Our accomplishments are God's accomplishments
Our gifts are God's gifts
Our talents are God's talents
What we do—we do through him

Our success is God's success
What we do—we do for him

~Introduction~

Let's face it... life is tough. With a reminder of what's important and that life is just a place, we can better manage through life's obstacles, setbacks and difficulties.

It is so easy to get caught up in the day to day routines, the desire to make something great of ourselves and the competition we create against life itself, that we forget the true meaning of life. That true meaning is the relationship we have with God and others and the beauty and peace in each and every day.

Life has a way of pushing us to self-fulfillment, self-gratification and self-pity. Life has a way of creating so much noise that we often forget where to find peace. We seek retreats and solace through vacations and enjoyment of material things, when true peace and tranquility comes from just being still and embracing the moment of being calm, of just taking in life by breathing and letting everything else go.

This collection of poems will hopefully remind you of the importance of life and that it is just a moment of our time. Life is a place to learn, love and eventually let go. It is not our forever and when that perspective is taken it is much easier to live. Our forever is so much more.

Rolling Horizon, ©2012 PhotosbyMeredith

Understanding

In myself I must **BELIEVE**
It's the way to achieve
God's plan for me has much in store
For my purpose–there's so much more

LOVE God first before all else
Next our neighbors before ourselves
A kind heart is the way to be
To live a life that's satisfying

Take time to read God's every word
LISTEN to the wisdom I have heard
God has given us a guide
He won't forsake us–he's by our side

God is caring and gave us **GRACE**
So all the trials we can face
He knows that we all will sin
He will forgive again—and again

In my heart I know the **TRUTH**
That I am special and so are you
God made me just how I should be
That's all I need to live happily

FAITH in God's plan is the key
To an open mind so I can see
He will provide and lead the way
To fulfill my purpose every day

Understanding and Other Poems

This collection of poems has been divided into the six key themes of the poem *Understanding* in an effort to reinforce focal points for our life and to remind us of the value of our journey in this world.

The six key areas of focus are:

BELIEVE — believe in yourself and God's purpose for you.

LOVE — love God and others before yourself.

LISTEN — listen to God's word, wisdom and guidance.

GRACE — remember God's grace, caring nature and sacrifice for our sins.

TRUTH — acknowledge the truth and happiness within ourselves.

FAITH — have faith in God's plan.

Each poem wasn't written specifically for each area, but was written as an outcome of a specific issue, challenge or setback going on in my life or the lives of those around me. By placing these poems in this format it will hopefully add some additional value and perspective to the key areas. The main goal, though, is to instill hope, encouragement and inspiration. I hope you enjoy them as much as I have.

~Believe~

In myself I must **BELIEVE**
It's the way to achieve
God's plan for me has much in store
For my purpose–there's so much more

Being confident of this very thing, that he which hath begun a good work in you will perform it until the day of Jesus Christ.

—Philippians 1:6

Many are the plans in the mind of a man, but it is the purpose of the Lord that will stand.

—Proverbs 19:21 (ESV)

For I know the thoughts that I think toward you, saith the Lord, thoughts of peace, and not of evil, to give you an expected end.

—Jeremiah 29:11

For we are his workmanship, created in Christ Jesus for good works, which God prepared beforehand, that we should walk in them.

—Ephesians 2:10 (ESV)

Such is the confidence that we have through Christ toward God. Not that we are sufficient in ourselves to claim anything as coming from us, but our sufficiency is from God, who has made us sufficient to be ministers of a new covenant, not of the letter but of the Spirit.

—2 Corinthians 3:4–5 (ESV)

Believe—believe in ourselves and God's purpose for us.

Everyone wants different things out of life, but I am certain that there is one thing that we all desire that is the same and that is happiness. Happiness comes from knowing that you are loved and taken care of and that someone is looking out for you. That someone is God. God created all of us for a purpose and a reason. Since he did create each of us with individual talents and skills and for an individual purpose and plan in mind there is no doubt that God believes in us and the abilities he has instilled in us. It is not always easy to understand the reason God has chosen us to be where we are at any given point in time, but God understands. Just as it isn't always easy to know when and how we are being used, God has a reason and a purpose for each moment of our life. You can believe in God's plan and purpose and feel assured that you are where you are at any given point in time because that is where you are meant to be. That is why it is important to believe in the plan God has for you. When stepping back and looking at your situation in this perspective, it can really change your attitude, behaviors and focus in life.

Whether you feel you are in a good place and everything seems to be falling in line or if you feel you are in a difficult time of your life and don't seem to have any answers, it is reassuring to know that God has a reason for you at this moment in this particular time of your life. Most likely there is a lesson to be learned by whatever you are going through or you are where you are to help someone else and the difficulties they are facing.

One thing we should remember is life is not about us, it is about others and God's plan. It is so easy to get caught up in the "me" and the "now", but it is really about so much more—God's purpose for our life. Even if we haven't chosen to be a part of it, guess what—we already are.

An amazing thing happens when you start to believe in yourself. I have seen this personally in my life. It has always been a struggle to believe in myself. But during moments and periods of time when I have, truly amazing things have happened.

Often there is so much noise around us that keeps us from the truth which is that we are truly valuable and important in this world. It seems that there are always plenty of people to remind us that we are not, to criticize or just flat put us down but it is so important not to let these words of discouragement keep us from believing in what is really true—you are valuable—you are important—you are you for a reason.

"I was a Nobody, until I realized that I have always been a Somebody."

—C. L. Saltz

Dreams, ©2012 C. L. Saltz

Dreams...

Are the thoughts…
Wispily floating through your mind

Are always building…
Like a fresh summer storm

Are growing…
To become larger each day

Are very powerful…
Controlling all actions and emotions

Are our desires…
Secrets within the heart

Are often aching…
To be so much more

Are the possibilities…
When pursued into reality

Are fulfillment…
When finally reached

Dreams… are the
Cornerstone of happiness

Be The You, You Want to Be

Why can't you be
The way you are
With thoughts drifting
Someplace far

Why can't you be
Something more
The someone you wish
And often long for

Be bold and brave
Hold strong and fast
Be confident and sure
With a will that will last

Be smarter and able
Be courageous and true
Be the desired self
Be the real you

For if you can envision
And picture the dream
Then there's no reason why
You can't be more than it seems

It takes a belief
And a little faith
In your abilities
To be something great

If others can do it
Then why not you
There's no difference
In what people can do

The only difference
That helps others succeed
Is the faith they have
In their ability

So why not be the you
That you really want to be
It starts with your choice
And desire to believe

Trust, ©2012 C. L. Saltz

Trust

Go ahead said my friend
You can trust me 'til the end
So I took a step, gently
Until I felt more carefree

It's okay to let go
I am here to watch you, as you grow
I start to dream and start to fly
I count the days as they pass by

You are special and you are bright
You must believe with all your might
I'm like a climber on the edge
But have full faith and soul to pledge

Just take the leap; a leap of faith
You have the skill; and what it takes
With such a friend, I'll do what I must
It's because of you; someone I trust

You had it in you all along
To find the tune to your own song
And so I found the way for me
To succeed and live happily

The Best You

You may not be good enough
To make first string
Although you work harder
Than the rest of your team

You may not be good enough
To catch that one person's eye
Although you made the effort
And continued to try

You may not be good enough
Per your boss at work
Although you work hard
The tasks you don't shirk

When it comes right down to it
Who are you trying to please
You'll never be good enough
For those you want to appease

Because it is not really about
Being good enough for others to accept
It's about being satisfied with you
When you're truly adept

When you try your best
But don't make the cut
You should feel proud of your efforts
Don't fall into a rut

If you have truly done your best
Then there's not more you can do
You've got to keep moving on
And be proud to just be you

Life's just too hard
To please others always
You have to be satisfied
With yourself each day

There's one opinion that matters
When your efforts are true
And he will be pleased
When you are The Best You

Believe

So in the pit of despair
It is nice to know something is there
For in myself I should have faith
That I can seek and find the way

I am okay, it must be true
For if I'm not, there's not much to do
I can't change my looks or my face
For to try to do so is just a chase

I should be happy with who I am
So when I'm alone I can stand
Enjoy myself and my own way
God is with me every day

He is the one that made me—me
It is my turn to only see
That I'm okay—I'm alright
I can make it—it's all in sight

Soaring, ©2012 C. L. Saltz

Breaking Free

One of these days
I will soar
I will break through these walls
And find so much more

I'll be set free
And find my way
It will finally be
My special day

It's only a matter of time
Before I'm there
I will be free
To go anywhere

No longer held
By these chains
Freedom calls
And it rings

It is my time
Just wait and see
I will be more
Than even thought to be

It's only a matter of time
Before I'm there
I will be free
To go anywhere

My time is now
My time—it is now
I'm free...

Masterpiece, ©2012 C. L. Saltz

Mold Your Own Way

If tomorrow was but
A pile of clay
It would seem much easier
To mold your day

You could create something
That resembled art
And if you wished
You could make a new start

Each day you could mold
A new beginning
In case you didn't like
Where you were ending

You could sculpt
And design a masterpiece
That would make life fulfilling
And you more at ease

...

It would be all up
To only you
To determine how the day
Would turn out, too

If only each day
Could be molded like this
Life would be easy
And never amiss

But really there isn't
Any reason why
Each day couldn't be molded
If you're willing to try

You are the artist
And you have the tools
To mold your day
And make your own rules

If it's a masterpiece
That you're longing to find
Mold your own way
Life's for you to design

The real creator
Has made you the clay
For you to go
And mold your own way

He made each one
Special and pure
With talents and skills
To help us endure

It's up to us
To use all that he gave
To create a life
To mold our own way

Looking Back, ©2012 C. L. Saltz

Looking Back

When I grow up
I hope to be
Something that is
Completely amazing

I want to make
A difference
And make
My life count

I want to do
Great things
And for my efforts
To amount

For others to see
That I really did care and
For others to be better
For having me there

I want to be needed
And accepted too
For anything, everything
And all that I do

I just want to look back
On my life someday
And know that I did my best
To follow God's way

I want to be challenged
Pushed to succeed
And accomplish hopes, desires
And most of all dreams

I want to be able
To look back with a smile
To know I did all I could
To cross that last mile

I hope to not ever have
One single regret
For missing a chance
I'll never forget

There is a way to ensure
My dreams do come true
I must believe and take action
To see it all through

~Love~

LOVE God first before all else
Next our neighbors before ourselves
A kind heart is the way to be
To live a life that's satisfying

The fruit of the righteous is a tree of life; and he that winneth souls is wise.

—Proverbs 11:30

There is no fear in love; but perfect love casteth out fear: because fear hath torment. He that feareth is not made perfect in love.

—1 John 4:18

And we know that all things work together for good to them that love God, to them who are the called according to his purpose.

—Romans 8:28

Thou shalt not avenge, nor bear any grudge against the children of thy people, but thou shalt love thy neighbour as thyself: I am the Lord.

—Leviticus 19:18

The Lord is slow to anger and abounding in steadfast love, forgiving iniquity and transgression, but he will by no means clear the guilty, visiting the iniquity of the fathers on the children, to the third and fourth generation.

—Numbers 14:18 (ESV)

And thou shalt love the Lord thy God with all thine heart, and with all thy soul, and with all thy might.

—Deuteronomy 6:5

Companions, ©2013 C. L. Saltz

Love—love God and others before yourself.

Love is an interesting thing. When it comes to people, pets, things that fall within our own little world it is so easy to love. But when it comes to those we meet along a sidewalk, neighbors down the street, and especially those who are on the other side of the world, our love doesn't stretch that far.

We prefer to spend our time and money on things that affect "our" world as opposed to sharing the things

God provides to reach others. We often get so wrapped up in the "things" life provides that we forget that it is truly the people around us that make life meaningful. I am guilty of just letting life happen and looking the other way when something is going on. It is easy to throw a few dollars at a cause instead of taking the time to really get involved. I am still trying to learn how to be a better servant than my own master. I know there is so much I could be doing and it takes a constant effort to focus our time and energy on things that really matter and can make a difference.

Life is a gift bestowed on us by God and love is how we show our gratitude. Love is as simple as taking the time to listen, to making the right choices and saying the right things to others, to overlooking others mistakes and flaws and helping them overcome their obstacles. If there was more love in this world it could be such a wonderful place.

Storyteller, ©2012 C. L. Saltz

The Storyteller

There once was a quiet man
That would stop by every day
He was always very patient
And there was always lots to say

Our conversations were long
And around many things they would venture
I was always eager to share
And to describe my every adventure

He would often nod his head
And throw in a comment or two
We had such a glorious time
Like the time now here, with you

I became so very fond
Of these moments in time we spent
As I look back even now, it's clear
He must have been heaven sent

As the days passed on by
And our friendship grew ever strong
I longed for the time we spent
It was where I seemed to belong

But then there came a day
When my friend, he did not show
I realized at once, however
That his name I didn't know

For all those times we sat
And chatted each and every day
It was he that always listened
While I had all to say

I looked and searched all over
To find someone else he knew
I was amazed at what I learned
And that I had no clue

For my very special friend
Had such an amazing past
If I had only stopped long enough
The treasures I would have grasped

There are things he could have told me
And things I could have learned
If I had only been more willing
To give my friend a turn

But I didn't seem to notice
I was preoccupied with myself
And now I've missed an opportunity
To increase my knowledge wealth

Although I didn't listen well
My friend did teach me a lot
With silence, patience and kindness
I would experience the life that is sought

I also finally realized
The value we all provide
For we all have a story
That is waiting to come alive

So what is it you can tell me
And what is on your mind
For you are the storyteller
For you, I will make the time

The Mirage, ©2012 C. L. Saltz

The Mirage

Life is a mirage
My eyes play tricks on me
For they want me to believe
What I want them to see

I sit beside many others
As I set out for my destination
Not bothering to learn about
Those who share my transportation

Walking down the sidewalk
I nod at those I meet
But fail to lift a hand
To those sitting at my feet

I find a special cause
To give a routine donation
But what else can I be doing
To improve this world and nation

Life is a mirage
My eyes play tricks on me
For they want me to believe
What I want them to see

I don't know what I stand for
For I fail to take a stand
I'm so used to walking onward
I choose to just pretend

But the day will finally come
When I have to pay my dues
And I'll want someone to notice
And not pretend they have no clue

But why should they bother
If I wasn't ever strong
Why should they even care
If I never did belong

Life is a mirage
My eyes play tricks on me
For they want me to believe
What I want them to see

I need to make some sense
Of the mirage in front of me
I have to find my purpose
So I can finally see

There is a reason why I'm here
And stand right here with you
I need to trust the reason why
And the task that I must do

For if I do what's right
And help others out today
Then others will return the favor
When it is me in need one day

We all will find ourselves one day
In need a time or two
Wouldn't it be so great
To find a friend right here with you

Life's mirage will then become
A clear picture that I see
My purpose I will have served
And will have met my destiny

Imagine, ©2012 C. L. Saltz

Imagine

Imagine the world
It's a much better place
Where we all work together
The same hurdles we face

We take the time
To show others we care
We look for a way
To help and to share

We treat each other
With their due respect
We value ideas
And find ways to connect

We don't steal; we don't cheat
And we surely don't lie
We understand each other
We make an effort to try

We are always there
To lend others a hand
It's a choice we make
Because we all understand

Life is not easy
It is challenging at most
But we can't give up
And we can't choose to coast

For there are too many who
Have decided to not try
They would prefer that others
Work harder to help them get by

If we would all decide
To do our own part
And all help each other
To make a fresh start

We all have the ability
To succeed in our own way
We must make an effort
For each brighter day

It won't be easy
No one said that it would
But we all have a purpose
And that's understood

We can realize the circle
We are all running around
Could be a path instead
That leads up and not down

It's great to imagine
This wonderful thing
But actions are necessary
For true change to bring

So what are you doing
Still reading this page
Take the first step
And go make a change

Negotiation, ©2014 C. L. Saltz

Live Together

Why can't we all just
Learn to live together
Share each other's space
And learn to share the day

We often appear to
Like one another
And then in the next moment
We just look away

We don't stop to help one another
We don't offer to lend a hand
We just walk on by, like we don't see
We waste no time as we pretend

Why can't we all just
Learn to live together
Share each other's space
And learn to share the day

We fill our life with only our self
We look out for just one thing
We fail to see the purpose
And we miss life's meaning

Life's so much more than one person
And so much more than one's dreams
There's a whole world of many others
Who are just looking for simple things

Why can't we all just
Learn to live together
Share each other's space
And learn to share the day

Helping others and lending a hand
Is the one thing we should do
It is our goal and purpose
The one thing to see us through

So do what's right and stop
What is it you can do
Take a minute, take a step
Put one foot in front of you

For after a moment
You will be walking a straight line
You will be making a difference
That will last for all time

We can all
Live together
Sharing our space
Sharing our day

C. L. Saltz

Everyone Needs Someone

Someone to look up to
And one who will care
Someone who will be there
For your thoughts to share

It's important to build
Relationships that are strong
It's the one thing to help
Feel like you belong

A certain someone
A special friend
Someone to lean on
A friend 'til the end

Someone who knows
Your innermost thoughts
Someone to support you
When you have your doubts

Someone you can trust
Who you can confide in
Someone who will be there
When you need a friend

It's nice to have
Someone to lean on
To get through the day
When each day is done

Everyone needs someone
This much is true
You can't do it alone
Nor shouldn't want to

So here's to life's
Special true friends
Who will always be there
'Til the very end

Friends, ©2012 C. L. Saltz

Untrue Friendship

I thought you were a friend
Wished that it were true
For you to care for me
As much as I for you

There is a simple fact
That is abundantly true
It was my soul that I poured out
While yours, I never knew

I enjoyed our time together
And the chats we had each day
But I did all the talking
You had not much to say

I wanted you to pick up the phone
To give me a call
But my phone did not ring
That's when I knew it all

The friendship I thought we had
Well, I was just mistaken
It wasn't what it seemed
For me, I was forsaken

I thought that you might send
Just a tiny little note
It wouldn't be a long one
Just a few nice words you wrote

There was no call nor a note
That came from you today
And so I'm left wondering
What is my own way

I really thought that you would
Show me that you cared
Especially at this time
When I am sad and scared

And just when I thought
I could figure out no more
There you stand patiently
Waiting at my door

You thought instead of calling
You would stop by to say hello
Not what I had been thinking or
The emotions I let show

Neighbors, ©2012 C. L. Saltz

Neighbors

Down the block I take a stroll
And there I stop to see
The ashes of a neighbor's house
Who lived right next to me

It creates a lot of emotion
And there I stop to ponder
We lived next door for years
But I have to stop and wonder

I would often go and raise a hand
Or stop to say hello
But I never really took the time
To really get to know

I always saw the things
That I really wanted to see
But never really took the time
To see everything in front of me

I was always very busy
With lots of things on my mind
I didn't want to impose
I didn't think I had the time

But now I wonder why
I failed to get to know
These friends next to me
My heart I failed to show

One thing that is certain
With each step that I do make
I am right here today
It is a step I long to take

For it is never truly late
To stop and lift a hand
To smile at an acquaintance
To ease the burden of a friend

It is why that I am here
For I need to endure
I am meant to be a friend
And to love my neighbor

But there is a little more
To completely do the math
A neighbor isn't just next door
But everyone within our path.

~Listen~

Take time to read God's every word
LISTEN to the wisdom I have heard
God has given us a guide
He won't forsake us–he's by our side

Trust in the Lord with all your heart, and do not lean on your own understanding. In all your ways acknowledge him, and he will make straight your paths.

—Proverbs 3: 5–6 (ESV)

If any of you lacks wisdom, let him ask God, who gives generously to all without reproach, and it will be given him.

—James 1:5 (ESV)

My son, if you receive my words and treasure up my commandments with you, making your ear attentive to wisdom and inclining your heart to understanding; yes, if you call out for insight and raise your voice for understanding, if you seek it like silver and search for it as for hidden treasures, then you will understand the fear of the Lord and find the knowledge of God. For the Lord gives wisdom; from his mouth come knowledge and understanding.

—Proverbs 2: 1–6 (ESV)

Draw near to God, and he will draw near to you.

—James 4:8 (ESV)

Happy is the man that findeth wisdom, and the man that getteth understanding.

—Proverbs 3:13

Reassurance, ©2012 C. L. Saltz

Listen—listen to God's word, wisdom and guidance.

Go to any bookstore and you will find books among books with an effort to help us seek the meaning of life, to find our purpose, to solve our problems. There is only one book that exists that can provide the true answers and it is amazing the time and money we spend on other sources. The Bible provides the answers of how we should live our life, for the understanding of life and for the direction we should follow.

We fool ourselves into thinking that there are other answers, and that if we just continue looking we will find them. When we read and seek understanding through God's word, we can gain accurate perspective for our life and purpose.

In addition, if we stop to listen to the message God sends us through everyday interactions then we can follow his guidance and the path he has created for us.

Retirement, ©2013 C. L. Saltz

Retirement

Won't it be grand
Won't it be great
When retirement comes
I can hardly wait

Some folks save
And put money away
But it's not necessary
For this special day

I can feel the freedom
And the joy it will bring
When retirement comes
I can feel my heart sing

Every day will be filled
With a warm ocean breeze
The sun will always shine
I will feel so at ease

There will be friends
And family too
To share in laughter
And loving times too

Each day I will vacation
At a tropical place
With coconuts and palm trees
A breeze in my face

There will be laughter and fun
All of the time
Never sadness or loneliness
I will always be fine

Retirement will be
The most wonderful thing
True happiness will finally
Be the one thing it will bring

I can finally stop worrying
About life's trivial things
Because the retirement I long for
Will not include such things

The retirement I mention
Earth is not where I reside
I will be up in Heaven
With the Lord by my side

Next Generation, ©2013 PhotosbyMeredith

Alone No More

There is silence in the air
If only there was someone
But there is no one to care
I am alone

I reach out to fill the void
And am met by a voice
I stop to say hello
But then the wind does blow

Just when I thought I met a friend
It turned out to be the wind
I turn to look around
Surprised by what I found

I realize yet again
I am on my own
With no one around
I was all alone

I longed and hoped before the end
That I would somewhere find a friend
I needed someone to walk with me
As I went through my life's journey

And then I felt it and heard it too
That maybe there was something true
I heard a whisper and felt the breeze
The wind suddenly put me at ease

The voice and wind I felt before
Will be with me forevermore
As long as there is a breeze, you see
I'll have a friend that walks with me

Right Where I Belong

I am stuck out in the rain
Right where I belong
With patience I will listen
To the rain and to its song

I could be broken hearted
About the rain coming down on me
But it wouldn't do any good
It is where I'm meant to be

I could look around and wish
That I was someplace dry
But then I would miss out
On the lesson that would pass me by

There is something wonderful
About each and every thing
Sometimes we fail to stand still
And value the gift that it may bring

We want to jump ahead
To the next place in our life
Instead of embracing the moment
To understand all our strife

As we go through the obstacles
Life brings to us each day
We should learn to understand
The role that it might play

As we learn and gain wisdom
By the challenges we encounter
We step a little closer
To the purpose within our power

Even if you are
In a very difficult spot
Life becomes easier knowing
This isn't your final lot

There is a plan and purpose
That one day will come true
And all the hardships that you faced
Were there to see you through

Without all the knowledge
You learned each and everyday
You wouldn't have been able
To stand outside in the rain

So when you find yourself stuck
Someplace that feels all wrong
Perhaps you need to look again
You might be right where you belong

Peace, ©2013 C. L. Saltz

Peace

If you listen
You can hear
The tranquil peace
That is so near

It takes patience
And a calmness too
So that you can really
Feel the peace within you

Don't let your thoughts
Lead you astray
They are so very often
Just lies anyway

Because the things
We tell ourselves
Were just made up
And cause us to fail

We let the smallest
Trivial things
Become our purpose
Giving them meaning

That is why
We need to see
We should change
Where our focus will be

For when we choose
To tell the truth
Peace will be there
A quiet within you

Insight, ©2013 C. L. Saltz

Insight

What a waste of time
Searching for knowledge and truth
It's what we seek after
From the days of our youth

Every day we look harder
We look high and look low
We read all we can find
So that knowledge we'll know

We buy all the latest
The bestselling books
We want every advantage
From life's determined experts

We keep on searching
Through each day and night
To gain understanding
And lots of insight

It's actually quite funny
To see what we will do
To gain a small edge
To distance me from you

We are so eager
We fail to see
That the truth is so simple
It's really hard to believe

It is there waiting for us
Pure knowledge to gain
But because it's so simple
And brings with it no pain

We miss the chance
And the opportunity
To seek out the truth
For you and for me

We don't give the credit
Or faith that it deserves
We keep seeking and looking
Peeking around each single curve

It's like the search
For the fountain of youth
In hope that there is somewhere
A fountain of truth

We are so lucky
Because one does exist
We can stop to drink
And bathe in the mist

It is not exclusive
To the special elite
But is very elusive
To those who don't see

It is right there for all
Who will take the time to read
Pure knowledge of life
Answers of how we succeed

I could tell you the answer
But most would just scoff
They don't have the faith
That one book is enough

But that is the answer
To your life long quest
Go for it my friend
Go be my guest

~Grace~

God is caring and gave us **GRACE**
So all the trials we can face
He knows that we all will sin
He will forgive again–and again

The Lord is gracious, and full of compassion; slow to anger, and of great mercy.

—Psalm 145:8

For I am sure that neither death nor life, nor angels nor rulers, nor things present nor things to come, nor powers, nor height nor depth, nor anything else in all creation, will be able to separate us from the love of God in Christ Jesus our Lord.

—Romans 8:38–39 (ESV)

Fear thou not; for I am with thee: be not dismayed; for I am thy God: I will strengthen thee; yea, I will help thee; yea, I will uphold thee with the right hand of my righteousness.

—Isaiah 41:10

In the day of prosperity be joyful, but in the day of adversity consider: God also hath set the one over against the other, to the end that man should find nothing after him.

—Ecclesiastes 7:14

And let the peace of Christ rule in your hearts, to which indeed you were called in one body. And be thankful.

—Colossians 3:15 (ESV)

God is our refuge and strength, a very present help in trouble.

—Psalm 46:1

But he said to me, "My grace is sufficient for you, for my power is made perfect in weakness." Therefore I will boast all the more gladly of my weaknesses, so that the power of Christ may rest upon me. For the sake of Christ, then, I am content with weaknesses, insults, hardships, persecutions, and calamities. For when I am weak, then I am strong.

—2 Corinthians 12:9–10 (ESV)

I know your works. Behold, I have set before you an open door, which no one is able to shut. I know that you have but little power, and yet you have kept my word and have not denied my name.

—Revelation 3:8 (ESV)

Grace—remember God's grace, caring nature and sacrifice for our sins.

God is a loving God, but he is also a strict God. He expects obedience and loyalty to him. He loves us and will reward us for that faithfulness. God is full of grace. Grace for all of his children and for the human characteristics that we are burdened with. God provides grace to forgive us when we fail to have the courage to do the right thing or fail to react in a way that is Christ-like.

God provided the ultimate sacrifice for us by sending his son to die for our sins. It is through this act of pure love that we can be assured of God's grace. It is through these actions that we should desire to love those around us and to encourage others and not find fault in them. It should encourage us to be the best we can be. Take time to listen to God and to believe in him.

Child of Mine

Come my child
It is your time
I want you here
To be by my side

You've done everything
You were sent for
Now you'll be with me
Forevermore

Your life on earth
Was but a moment in time
An eternity awaits
Child of mine

There are much bigger things
For you in store
As you sit beside me
Forevermore

Sometimes loved ones
Who are left behind
Don't always see
What I have in mind

It's not always easy
From their point of view
To understand the purpose
I have for you

But know this my child
You will be fine
I love you so much
Child of mine

Hope, ©2012 C. L. Saltz

Hope

There it is, I just saw it
To look away will be to miss it
Sometimes not visible by human sight
You have to search with all your might

There again it just passed by
A glimmer, shimmer throughout the sky
It's quick—it's here and then it's gone
It's like it's unsure where to belong

It's searching, looking for a home
Perhaps I need it, I'm all alone
It sounds too great a risk for me
To think there is eternity

But yet that is what I've been told
In God, believe and to stay bold
That doesn't mean that I still know
How to live the life you did show

I am lost and cannot see
That sliver of hope awaiting me
Grief and despair are a way of life
But your grace will overcome and then suffice

For now I know it will be okay
For you have come and led the way
I can see it—it's brighter still
Hope remains—it is your will.

Grove Under, ©2013 PhotosbyMeredith

What If

What if you look back
At decisions you've made
And realize the results
You would easily trade

There were too many choices
That were not thought through
The decisions you made
Were not the real you

Maybe you let others
Convince what you said
And talked you into
The things that you did

What if you look back
At things you have done
And realize the hurt
Can't be undone

You didn't care back then
About those you had hurt
Or even the consequences
For treating others like dirt

You chose the wrong path
But there is no stopping
You can't go back now
You've got to keep walking

But what if there is
Yet another way to go
It is not backwards
But a new path to follow

This way leads to
A straight certain path
With a guide who will lead
Through all aftermath

And what if I told you
That there is no cost
Because the toll has been paid
By one other's loss

God sent his son Jesus
To die on the cross
So our poor decisions
For us would not cost

It only takes a belief
That all this is true
For you to move down the path
God created for you

Wanderer, ©2013 C. L. Saltz

Wanderer

Where is it I am going
And what am I supposed to do
I am so uncertain
And really have no clue

You would think that I would know
And have some great big plan
But I really don't know where to go
And I just don't understand

I feel so very inadequate
And often times alone
I wish there were a map for me
To guide me to some place known

I feel like each passing day
Is another one I have lost
If I only knew where I'd end up
I'd know what each day has cost

It seems to me each day that's past
Is a large waste of my time
For if I don't know where I'll end up
Are my efforts really mine

I am longing for some answers
And one day they will come
I just hope there is plenty of time
And my story's not yet done

For I want to have a purpose
And a reason for being here
And to see that there's a meaning
And nothing at all to fear

It will be nice to realize some day
When the path I take has ended
The choices that I made each day
Were the ones that were intended

Aloneness

It's so hard to go it alone
When you're not sure where to go
It's hard to stay strong and focused
And sometimes it's just hard to know

The confidence doesn't always come
And it is hard to stay motivated
But my heart can't be crushed so easy
And my goals are not dissipated

I am strong because I've done this before
And I have a will to succeed
I am determined and strong and won't stop
Until I find my need

I work hard and I am focused
I will keep looking for signs that are new
Things to make me notice
That the path I'm on is true

I may be alone in time
But I'm not alone in the end
I will always have God to rely on
With Him there's no need to pretend

Aloneness is a state of mind
That distracts me occasionally
But it doesn't stop the plans I have
To keep going each day and succeed

112   *Understanding and Other Poems*

Closed Opening, ©2013 PhotosbyMeredith

Trapped

I'm trapped in a world
That's unforgiving
Trapped in a world
That doesn't share

Trapped in a world
Where there's no living
Trapped in a world
That doesn't care

There are bars
On the windows
And a chain
Across the door

There's no music
Or salvation
There's only concrete
On the floor

I'm trapped in a world
That's unforgiving
Trapped in a world
That doesn't share

Trapped in a world
Where there's no living
Trapped in a world
That doesn't care

I'm tired of having
No where I can go
And I'm tired
Of all these chains

I'm tired
Of always thinking
And I'm tired
Of all these pains

I'm trapped in a world
That's unforgiving
Trapped in a world
That doesn't share

Trapped in a world
Where there's no living
Trapped in a world
That doesn't care

I can't stay
Here waiting
Hoping one day
Things will change

I've got to make
A difference
So I can get
Rid of these chains

I'm trapped in a world
That's unforgiving
Trapped in a world
That doesn't share

Trapped in a world
Where there's no living
Trapped in a world
That doesn't care

So I will take a stand
To really care
And I will take a stand
To be strong

It's my faith in God
That will get me through
And help me each day
To carry on

I'm trapped in a world
That's unforgiving
Trapped in a world
That doesn't share

Trapped in a world
Where there's no living
Trapped in a world
That doesn't care

Seascape, ©2012 C. L. Saltz

A Sinner's Prayer

Dear Lord, oh God
Forgive me today
Forgive the things I do
Forgive the things I say

I try my best
I promise I really do
To walk down the path
Made especially by you

But sometimes there are days
When my best just isn't enough
And my actions and my words
My strength just isn't that tough

I know I was wrong
To lose my self-control
Over my thoughts and my actions
But that you already know

So I come to you and pray
And ask for your forgiveness
I will learn from my mistakes
To give you more and nothing less

You deserve the best me
It's the least that I can do
For you sent your son
So my life would be renewed

Thank you for being there
And patient always with me
I'm certainly a work in progress
But just you wait and see

I know I can be more
Of the person I should be
I will work so very hard
To prove that you can count on me

I know right from wrong
And how to take a stand
The importance of being patient
And not to make my own demands

You always know what's right
And the decision that's best for me
I must trust your plan
And rely on what I can't see

So thank you Lord again
For taking all this time
To watch over and care for me
I'm so glad that you are mine

~Truth~

In my heart I know the **TRUTH**
That I am special and so are you
God made me just how I should be
That's all I need to live happily

Look carefully then how you walk, not as unwise but as wise, making the best use of time, because the days are evil.

—Ephesians 5:15 (ESV)

Let not your hearts be troubled. Believe in God; believe also in me.

—John 14:1 (ESV)

Lead me, O LORD, in your righteousness because of my enemies; make your way straight before me.

—Psalms 5: 8 (ESV)

Lead me in your truth and teach me, for you are the God of my salvation; for you I wait all the day long.

—Psalms 25: 5 (ESV)

Love is patient and kind; love does not envy or boast; it is not arrogant or rude. It does not insist on its own way; it is not irritable or resentful; it does not rejoice at wrongdoing, but rejoices with the truth.

—1 Corinthians 13: 4–6 (ESV)

Truth—acknowledge the truth and happiness within ourselves.

Truth—this is the hardest thing for me to do. I give so much value to things that other people say and I let those things control my life. Input from others is important to improve ourselves; however not at the risk of letting your growth be hindered by harsh words, non-constructive criticism and just plain rude comments.

To really make the most of life it is important to find the truth in things we do and things others say. You have to realize when to listen and when to separate words of untruth. It takes the ability to look deep within you and know the value and truth to your own abilities, knowledge and being.

The inability to be strong in the truth of your own self can keep you from fulfilling the other areas focused on within this book: believing in ourselves; loving others; listening; focusing on God's grace; and having faith in God's plan.

Overtaking, ©2013 PhotosbyMeredith

Happiness

No one said
That tomorrow would come
And it doesn't matter
What's already done

Happiness comes
From this moment in time
From enjoying all the things
That I can call mine

God gave us everything
That we all will need
To live a life
That is full and carefree

We must remember
To not clutter it up
With all of life's trivial
Unnecessary stuff

He gave us this earth
That allows us to breathe
The animals and plants
That's how we succeed

It's important to remember
That there's not much more
That's really truly necessary
To add to this world

We all have ambitions
And desire many things
But these won't result
In what true happiness brings

It is more simple
Than we sometimes will see
True happiness is the relationship
Between him and me

The world is made up
Of such wonderful things
From the sunrise each morning
To the miracles he brings

We must take the time
Each single day
It's these things that matter
For happiness to stay

So next time life takes you
On an uncertain path
And you catch yourself wondering
Where true happiness is at

Just remember
This one simple thing
True happiness comes from
Each moment life brings

Transgression, ©2012 C. L. Saltz

War

There is a battle going on
It is raging all the time
There is nowhere to turn
There is nowhere to hide

It is complete chaos
The war that is going on
There will be no peace
Until the warring is finally done

But the battle that exists
Is one that tops the charts
It is fought day after day
Leaving many scars and marks

It puts a lot of pressure
To choose which side to pick
Which side should you be on
You must make your decision quick

Do you support the battle of truth
And strongly stand upright
Or do you choose the other side
Not sure which is right

The battle that rages on
Never seems to cease or stop
It continues all the time
With each decision and each thought

Regardless of all our effort
And every good intention
The enemy gains more ground
With every word that is mentioned

Because we tend to believe
All the lies we tell ourselves
The battle that rages on
Starts from the words out of our mouths

We are the ally
And we are the enemy
We fight among ourselves
For we fail to plainly see

We always look for things
That validates our fear
We remind ourselves each day
That success is never near

We tend to repeat these words
That we often tell ourselves
It is a path we have created
And one we've been led down

It is so much easier
To believe a lie than the truth
Because we have driven the lies
Into how we see our worth

But the battle must not go on
And we have to put an end
To all the lies and false truths
We should no longer pretend

We are who we are
And we can be who we want to be
If we would only believe
It's the first step before we see

That to win this final battle
That has gone on for many years
We need to believe in ourselves
And eliminate all of the fears

Presence, ©2014 C. L. Saltz

Lies

I told you a lie
When you stopped by today
When asked how I was doing
I said I was okay

But this was not the truth
It wasn't even close
Because my heart is sad
And it's friends I need the most

I always tend to hide
The true way that I feel
Because I never think
You want to know what's real

I always say I'm fine
As we pass by in the hall
But inside my heart is breaking
But blame—I take it all

For if you never knew
Exactly how I felt
Then how can I expect you to know
The problems I've been dealt

I lie about the truth
Because the truth is just a lie
I just can't seem to get it right
No matter how hard I try

I wear a heavy armor
To protect my inner soul
While inside there's a china doll
Breaking from its mold

I guess it's up to me now
To let you know how I feel
So you can be there for me
I know our friendship's real

Open Unto You, ©2013 PhotosbyMeredith

Get Your Cheer On

Walking through life
Can be a difficult challenge
All the obstacles that are faced
Is sometimes hard to imagine

It is hard enough
To just be you
But then add to that
A setback or two

It seems when you finally
Pull ahead of the race
Others are there
To put you back in your place

There are always those ones
Who enjoy to belittle
All the things that you do
Their words become critical

So instead of building up
People they love
They push them back down
So they don't rise above

That is the reason
You have to push on
Ignore harsh words
And get your cheer on

If you don't do it
Then tell me who will
Praise your strengths and your work
The truth to instill

If you listen to those
Who enjoy putting you down
You listen to lies
That will limit your bounds

You have to rise above
All the things people say
From them learn but don't let
Their words ruin your day

You have to keep moving
And trudging ahead
Don't hold yourself back
From the words that were said

Often times
I truly believe
The words aren't intentional
And meant to deceive

But it is what it is
And what's done is done
Don't dwell on those words
Instead get your cheer on

Think of it this way
When friends put you down
They are insecure
Of the success you have found

They are unintentionally
Keeping you back
From the growth that gets stopped
By their personal attack

You can't wait around
For others to be the one
Who build you up
So get your cheer on

You need to celebrate
The successes you have
Become your own cheerleader
And learn to be glad

Embrace your wins
And even the failures you make
That is just life
You get what you take

There is no one
To hold onto to your hand
You have to be strong
And learn how to stand

Don't wait around
For others to build you on up
Do it yourself
It's your winner's cup

Celebrate your successes
Don't put yourself down
Rise yourself up
And more success will abound

It takes constant focus
On the right things
Look ahead and not back
To what life will bring

The next race is there
Who cares where you place
As long as you participate
And join in the race

If you make the effort
And your best you have done
Then you are the winner
So Get Your Cheer On

Life's Real Meaning

Have you ever bought a car
And proudly drove it round
Pleased with yourself
And the new toy that you found

What about a brand new house
Built on the fresh cut dirt
Anxious to show it off
And to brag about its worth

The next thing that you know
You're thinking about these things
More often than you let yourself
Praise life's real meaning

You get totally caught up
In having something new
You lose sight and focus
And soon don't have a clue

You worry about your image
And who you hang around
Giving way too much importance
To the material things that you've found

Life tends to make it easy
To get caught up in all these things
We keep ourselves entangled
By all life's little strings

We often never stop
To remember the truth
Material things do not matter
It's love that provides our worth

For when we truly stop to show
How we love all that we can see
And how we love each other
Life will finally have meaning

Sunny Day, ©2011 C. L. Saltz

Rainy Day

Today when I awoke
It was a rainy day
The clouds were abundant
And the rain carried me away

The rain pounded on the rooftop
And numbed the thoughts inside my head
I curled up beneath the covers
The day I did dread

I was so reluctant
To step one foot out the door
The rain may be a flash flood
That would sweep me to the floor

Everything around me
Would be tossed all around
By all the current and water
That was swirling on the ground

I might get knocked off my feet
By something passing by
So I decide it might be best
Not to venture a single try

As I lay there so very cozy
Beneath the warm covers surrounding me
I began to see some sunlight
Peaking through the cloud debris

I began to wonder
If I stay inside my bed
All the things I would miss
While focused on all the dread

Sure I might be warm
Safe and comfortable
But I would be all alone
And might find myself miserable

And then I realized
That as soon as I would step outside
The clouds would finally break
And sunshine would be alive

It had been all up to me
To determine the weather for the day
As long as I was focused
On the right things along the way

Life, ©2011 C. L. Saltz

Life Is Just A Place

A place to make a friend
And build a family
But it doesn't stop with them
There's so much more you see

For we all are related
And should have each other's back
We should care about our neighbor
Not look for ways to attack

Life is just a place
Not the most important thing
For a life that's not well meant
Is a loss of its meaning

Life is just a place
A place to stop on through
For there's more around the corner
That's meant for me and you

Life is just a test
To see who can pass
It's important to listen
You can't retake the class

How many lives did we touch
How many souls did we save
Did we focus on just ourselves
Or was it our hearts that we gave

Did we stop to make a friend
Or rush ahead of those in line
Did we care about another
Did we bother to take the time

Life is just a place
A stopping point for me and you
For if we truly take the time
We would understand the truth

There is more that awaits
As we open the next door
I can't begin to imagine
What is totally in store

Life is just a place
Somewhere to see it through
For we all have a purpose
It's up to me and you

There's a goal and a need
For you and me today
For it is up to each of us
To help others find the way

We're here for a reason
If we look hard we will find
It is not to win the race
But help each other cross the line

~Faith~

FAITH in God's plan is the key
To an open mind so I can see
He will provide and lead the way
To fulfill my purpose every day

That your faith should not stand in the wisdom of men, but in the power of God.

—1 Corinthians 2:5

I can do all things through Christ which strengtheneth me.

—Philippians 4:13

Blessed is the man that endureth temptation: for when he is tried, he shall receive the crown of life, which the Lord hath promised to them that love him.

—James 1:12

Many are the afflictions of the righteous, but the Lord delivers him out of them all.

—Psalm 34:19 (ESV)

Count it all joy, my brothers, when you meet trials of various kinds, for you know that the testing of your faith produces steadfastness. And let steadfastness have its full effect, that you may be perfect and complete, lacking in nothing.

—James 1:2–4 (ESV)

What then shall we say to these things? If God is for us, who can be against us?

—Romans 8:31 (ESV)

Faith—have faith in God's plan.

What else is there to say…God does have a plan for us and when we decide to accept that and look for synchronicity in everyday life it all starts to make sense. If you look, there are small reassuring moments in life that reaffirm the direction or path that you may be on. And there are small reminders that God is there and watching over us.

It is easy to believe in God and his plan when things are going good but we tend to forget and start to feel sorry for ourselves when things are going bad. When we stop and look for solace during times of difficulty and take the time to consider the possibilities that there are reasons for the challenges we are faced with, we can put these into proper perspective. It could be that the difficulty we are facing is our chance to learn something new or learn how to deal with certain challenges to better prepare for the future. Even more important, it could be that the challenge we are facing allows us to help others who may go through the same issue. It could be that just by sharing our own stories with them we assist others in dealing with their own obstacles.

When you take challenges and obstacles and put them in perspective it can make these situations easier to live through. Also, when we stop to remember that life is just a place, it allows us to put all of our challenges in perspective. Typically in the scope of life, we tend to make much more of issues and challenges than if we step back and put each in its own perspective. We can realize that we shouldn't let our challenges manage us, we should manage our challenges.

God wants us to look to him for assistance through the obstacles life throws our way. Also, we should remember the truly important things in life and not worry about the trivial issues we are going through. When we do this we can keep things focused for our life and in perspective. God does have a plan and you are part of that plan. Knowing this should be enough to get through each and every day.

Wonder, ©2010 C. L. Saltz

It's Not Magic

He is not a magic maker
And he is not a mystery man
He is our God almighty
He makes miracles because he can

You may think he works his magic
Or works in mysterious ways
But just because we don't understand
Doesn't mean that is his way

He doesn't have a potion
And he doesn't hide what he can do
It should be so obvious
Because of the things in front of you

He is not a magic maker
And he is not a mystery man
He is our God almighty
He makes miracles because he can

He is so omnipotent
And completely powerful
He can make anything happen of course
He is the creator of this world

What is so very exciting
And so amazing to see
Is that he is willing to use his power
For even you and for me

He is not a magic maker
And he is not a mystery man
He is our God almighty
He makes miracles because he can

It happens everyday
Small miracles I do see
For I try to keep my eyes open
And see the things he does for me

It never seems to fail
The small things I always find
He is always right there watching
Just waiting to help in time

He is not a magic maker
And he is not a mystery man
He is our God almighty
He makes miracles because he can

It is so very clear
The power God does possess
It just takes a little faith
That is all and nothing less

Mazical, ©2010 C. L. Saltz

Mazical

It is up this way
Then back again
Don't look now
It's not the end

You go left
And then go right
You turn around
Just for spite

You can't hear
And you can't see
You don't even know
Where you're supposed to be

You try to run
And sometimes crawl
You hang on strong
So that you don't fall

The choices you've made
You'll never know
If the ones you took
Were the way to go

It's one step now
And later two
It's the very least
That you can do

For to completely stop
And never go
Will never lead
Where one can follow

So you will try as hard
As you can
So you may finally
Reach the end

Blending, ©2015 C. L. Saltz

Chameleon

I have a theory
And I have a plan
And I try real hard
To understand

I know just what
I should do
But don't spend enough time
Seeing it through

I get distracted
By life's little quirks
And end up most times
Being a jerk

I should spend more time
Doing what's right
And keeping the plan
In plain sight

Instead I catch myself
Following the crowd
Trying to blend in
To be a part of the now

When really these things
Aren't nearly enough
To fulfill the plan
I gotta be tough

I need to stay focused
Work hard and smart too
There is one key purpose
And thing I should do

I need not try
To be just another bloke
There is so much more
Life's just a joke

It's a distraction
An illusion to the eye
And I need not fall victim
Just continue to try

I've gotta learn
What comes first
If I choose right
I'll never thirst

By taking action
And making a stand
I can have it all
It'll be grand

I'm a chameleon
Most of the time
But with a little bit of focus
I'll stand out just fine

Chameleons adapt
And they blend in
But not much longer
'Tis true, my friend

Waterfall, ©2012 C. L. Saltz

I Look To You

I can't go it alone
I have tried
And things don't work out
So I look to you

I have big dreams
Are they yours or mine
I'm not sure
So I look to you

I try each day to do my best
But I don't know
When my best is enough
So I look to you

There's lots of choices
To make each day
I am not sure which to take
So I look to you

It seems that there isn't anyone
That cares enough to stay
That will listen to my thoughts
So I look to you

I trust you will be there
For me each and every day
I have the faith
So I look to you

I long for others too
But I know that it's okay
You have a plan and know me better anyway
So I look to you

I need to just let go
And follow your own way
It seems so easy to do
So I look to you

Give me the guidance
Give me the strength
Allow me to see
So I will always look to you

Heaven, ©2012 C. L. Saltz

Trip To Heaven

If it was my turn
To take a ride
And join so many others
Up in the sky

It would be fine
I would be okay
To know I was finally
On my way

I love my kids
And my family
But life's just so hard
To just be me

Heaven is the place
I long to be
Somewhere safe
Someplace free

I would never worry
And never fret
It's the one place
I would never forget

The days would be
Magical and sweet
Glorious and fine
A daily treat

Love would be
Everywhere I go
Friends all around
Everyone I would know

Mystified by all the
Things I would see
But understanding
Wisdom given to me

Awed by God's
Glorious site
Reverent fear
At his power and might

I can't wait
For that miraculous day
When earth becomes
A time far away

Stay on Track, ©2011 C. L. Saltz

What Does It Take to Succeed

What does it take to succeed?

Do I have it?
Can I learn it?
Can I get it?
Can I earn it?

What does it take to succeed?

Belief in one's self and ability
Positive thinking, a smile
Resilience each day
Some class and some style

What does it take to succeed?

Commitment and trust
Communication and teamwork
Dedication and strength
A little hard work

What does it take to succeed?

Others who are willing
To follow your lead
And lend you a hand
In your time of need

What does it take to succeed?

An open mind and
Be eager to grow
Seek ways to improve and
Increase what you know

What does it take to succeed?

A goal and a path
To start your journey
One step at a time
Will make life easy

What does it take to succeed?

All of these things
Are good for a while
And will help you get through
The very next mile

But what does it take
To really succeed
Faith in God's plan
For you and for me!

~Summary~

It all comes down to understanding that life is just a place.

So just...

BELIEVE — believe in yourself and God's purpose for you.

LOVE — love God and others before yourself.

LISTEN — listen to God's word, wisdom and guidance.

GRACE — remember God's grace, caring nature and sacrifice for our sins.

TRUTH — acknowledge the truth and happiness within ourselves.

FAITH — have faith in God's plan.

~About the Author~

C. L. Saltz has a full time career in Human Resource Management, specializing in organizational development, performance management and employee relations.

Educational experience includes a Bachelor of Science in Psychology and a Master of Science in Industrial / Organizational Psychology. Hobbies include spending time with family, travel, reading, writing and photography.

C. L. Saltz has an appreciation for nature and wildlife which serve as a reminder of God's creativity, power, love and wonder. C. L. Saltz can be reached at *clsaltzconnect@yahoo.com*.

www.ingramcontent.com/pod-product-compliance
Lightning Source LLC
Chambersburg PA
CBHW040415100526
44588CB00022B/2835